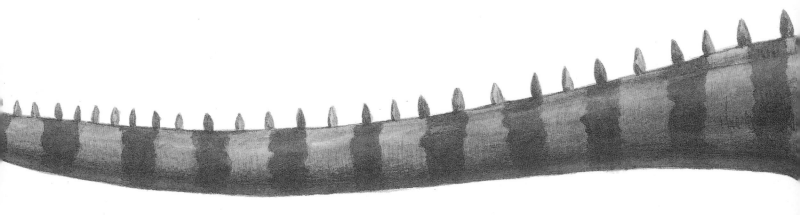

Dinosaur Feathers

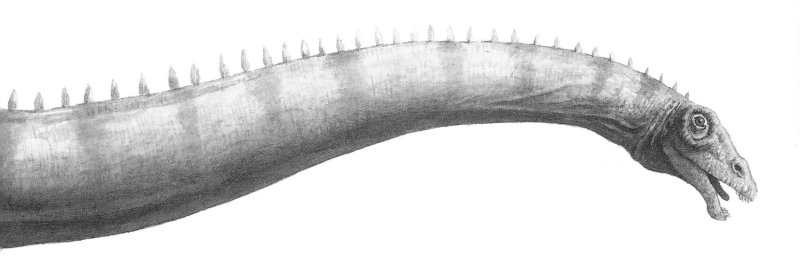

DENNIS NOLAN

NEAL PORTER BOOKS
HOLIDAY HOUSE / NEW YORK

The dinosaurs
Lived by the shores
Of Mesozoic seas.

And in the shade
Their eggs were laid
Among the ginkgo trees.

They ate the plants,
The worms, and ants.
They ate each other too.

With mighty roars
The dinosaurs
Just grew, and grew, and grew.

They roamed the land
And in the sand
They left behind their tracks.

Apatosaurus (uh-PAT-uh-sore-us),
Stegosaurus (STEH-guh-sore-us),
Saurophaganax (sore-uh-FAY-guh-nax),

Ceratosaurus (seh-RAT-oh-sore-us),
Allosaurus (AL-uh-sore-us),
Archaeopteryx (ar-kee-OP-ter-iks),

8

Mamenchisaurus (mah-MEN-chih-sore-us),
Kentrosaurus (KEN-truh-sore-us),
And Caudipteryx (kaw-DIP-teh-riks),

Ouranosaurus (ooh-RAN-uh-sore-us),

Gobisaurus (GO-bee-sore-us),

Hypsilophodon (hip-sih-LAH-fuh-don),

Amargasaurus (ah-MAR-guh-sore-us),

Qantassaurus (KWON-tuh-sore-us),

And Iguanodon (ih-GWHA-nuh-don),

11

Psittacosaurus (sih-TACK-uh-sore-us),

Spinosaurus (SPY-nuh-sore-us),

Just to name a few,

12

Velociraptor (ve-LAH-sih-rap-tor),
Oviraptor (OH-vih-rap-tor),
Maiasaura (MY-ah-sore-uh) too,

13

Einiosaurus (eye-NEE-oh-sore-us),

Gryposaurus (GRYE-puh-sore-us),

Pentaceratops (pen-tah-SER-uh-tops),

14

Ankylosaurus (ang-KEE-luh-sore-us),
Rajasaurus (RAH-jah-sore-us),
Protoceratops (pro-toh-SER-uh-tops),

15

Styracosaurus (sty-RAK-uh-sore-us),
Saltasaurus (SALT-uh-sore-us),
Edmontonia (ed-mon-TOE-nee-uh),

Tyrannosaurus (tih-RAN-uh-sore-us),
Carnotaurus (KAR-nuh-tore-us),
Borogovia (bore-uh-GOH-vee-uh),

17

With monstrous jaws
And fearsome claws,
They ruled the earth alone.

18

Then who knows why
They had to die.
Their bones were turned to stone.

Except a few
Whose feathers grew
And grew, and grew, and grew.

Flamingos, Owls,
Guineafowls,
And the Marabou.

21

They ate the bugs,
The seeds, and slugs.
They nested in the trees.

The Parakeets,
The Lorikeets,
The Wrens, and Chickadees.

23

And all day long
They sang their song.
They whistled, cawed, and cooed.

They chirped and cheeped,
They honked and peeped,
They cock-a-doodle-dooed.

25

The Ducks and Hawks,
The Gulls and Auks,
The Swan and Hummingbird.

26

Macaws and Quails,
Cranes and Rails,
And the Bowerbird.

27

The Frigatebird,
The Lyrebird,
The Loon and Cockatoo,

With squawks and cries
They filled the skies,
And flew, and flew . . .

And flew.

Pelecanimimus (PELL-eh-can-ih-mime-us) *Pelican mimic*, 6 ft. Europe, 135–125 mya	cover	Herrerasurus (her-RARE-uh-sore-us) *Herrera's lizard*, 15 ft. South America, 230 mya	page 3
Utahraptor (YEW-tah-rap-tor) *Thief from Utah*, 23 ft. North America, 130–125 mya	cover	Plateosaurus (PLAT-ee-uh-sore-us) *Flat lizard*, 26 ft. Europe, 205 mya	page 4
Microraptor (MY-crow-rap-tor) *Small thief*, 2½ ft. Asia, 128–124 mya	cover	Coelophysis (SEE-loh-fiss-iss) *Hollow form*, 10 ft. North America, 190 mya	page 4
Confuciusornis (kon-FEW-shus-or-nis) *Confucius bird*, 1½ ft. Asia, 125–120 mya	cover	Dilophosaurus (die-LOW-fuh-sore-us) *Two crested lizard*, 22 ft. Asia, North America, 195 mya	page 4
Shunosaurus (SHOO-nuh-sore-us) *Lizard from Shu*, 30 ft. Asia, 167–161 mya	endpaper	Yangchuanosaurus (yang-chew-AHN-uh-sore-us) *Lizard from Yangchuan*, 35 ft. Asia, 161–155 mya	page 5
Guanlong (gwan-LONG) *Crown dragon*, 10 ft. Asia, 160 mya	endpaper	Brachiosaurus (BRACK-ee-oh-sore-us) *Arm lizard*, 72 ft. Africa, North America, 153 mya	page 5
Diplodocus (dih-PLAH-duh-kus) *Double beam*, 80 ft. North America, 154–150 mya	page 1	Apatosaurus (uh-PAT-uh-sore-us) *Deceptive lizard*, 75 ft. North America, 145–150 mya	page 6
Eoraptor (EE-oh-rap-tor) *Dawn thief*, 5½ ft. South America, 230 mya	page 2	Stegosaurus (STEH-guh-sore-us) *Roofed lizard*, 21 ft. North America, 150 mya	page 6

The italicized phrases are translations of the Latin names.
Measurements represent the length from nose or beak to tip of tail.

32   mya=million years ago

Saurophaganax (sore-uh-FAY-guh-nax) *Ruler of the lizard eaters*, 35 ft. North America, 150 mya	page 7	
Ceratosaurus (seh-RAT-oh-sore-us) *Horned lizard*, 20 ft. North America, 153–148 mya	page 8	
Allosaurus (AL-uh-sore-us) *Different lizard*, 28 ft. North America, 155–150 mya	page 8	
Archaeopteryx (ar-kee-OP-ter-iks) *Ancient wing*, 1½ ft. Europe, 150–146 mya	page 8	
Mamenchisaurus (mah-MEN-chih-sore-us) *Lizard from Mamenchi*, 92 ft. Asia, 160–145 mya	page 9	
Kentrosaurus (KEN-truh-sore-us) *Pointed lizard*, 13 ft. Africa, 155–150 mya	page 9	
Caudipteryx (kaw-DIP-teh-riks) *Tail feather*, 2 ft. Asia, 136–125 mya	page 9	
Ouranosaurus (ooh-RAN-uh-sore-us) *Brave monitor lizard*, 27 ft. Africa, 125–112 mya	page 10	

Gobisaurus (GO-bee-sore-us) *Lizard from the Gobi Desert*, 20 ft. China, 125–99 mya	page 10
Hypsilophodon (hip-sih-LAH-fuh-don) *High-crested tooth*, 7 ft. Europe, 130–125 mya	page 10
Amargasaurus (ah-MAR-guh-sore-us) *Lizard from Amarga*, 43 ft. South America, 130–120 mya	page 11
Qantassaurus (KWON-tuh-sore-us) *Qantas (airlines) lizard*, 6 ft. Australia, 120–112 mya	page 11
Iguanodon (ih-GWHA-nuh-don) *Iguana tooth*, 26 ft. Europe, 120–112 mya	page 11
Psittacosaurus (sih-TACK-uh-sore-us) *Parrot lizard*, 6½ ft. Asia, 130–120 mya	page 12
Spinosaurus (SPY-nuh-sore-us) *Spine lizard*, 45 ft. Africa, 112–97 mya	page 12
Velociraptor (veh-LAH-sih-rap-tor) *Rapid thief*, 8 ft. Asia, 83–70 mya	page 13

Oviraptor (OH-vih-rap-tor) *Egg thief*, 5 ft. Asia, 83–72 mya	page 13	Styracosaurus (sty-RAK-uh-sore-us) *Spiked lizard*, 17 ft. North America, 77–73 mya — page 15
Maiasaura (MY-ah-sore-uh) *Good mother lizard*, 23 ft. North America, 83–70 mya	page 13	Saltasaurus (SALT-uh-sore-us) *Lizard from Salta*, 39 ft. South America, 70–66 mya — page 16
Einiosaurus (eye-NEE-oh-sore-us) *Buffalo (bison) lizard*, 19 ft. North America, 80–72 mya	page 14	Edmontonia (ed-mon-TOE-nee-uh) *Lizard from Edmonton*, 10 ft. North America, 80–66 mya — page 16
Gryposaurus (GRYE-puh-sore-us) *Hook-nosed lizard*, 25 ft. North America, 83–74 mya	page 14	Tyrannosaurus (tih-RAN-uh-sore-us) *Tyrant lizard*, 40 ft. North America, 68–66 mya — page 17
Pentaceratops (pen-tah-SER-uh-tops) *Five horned face*, 21 ft. North America, 80–72 mya	page 14	Carnotaurus (KAR-nuh-tore-us) *Meat-eating bull*, 25 ft. South America, 76–69 mya — page 17
Ankylosaurus (ang-KEE-luh-sore-us) *Fused lizard*, 23 ft. North America, 68–66 mya	page 15	Borogovia (bore-uh-GOH-vee-uh) *Borogove (from* Jabberwocky) 6½ ft. Asia, 85–66 mya — page 17
Rajasaurus (RAH-jah-sore-us) *King of lizards*, 35 ft. Asia, 70–66 mya	page 15	Tarbosaurus (TAR-boh-sore-us) *Alarming lizard*, 31 ft. Asia, 78–68 mya — page 18
Protoceratops (pro-toh-SER-uh-tops) *First-horned face*, 8 ft. Asia, 86–71 mya	page 15	Therizinosaurus (ther-uh-ZEEN-uh-sore-us) *Scythe lizard*, 33 ft. Asia, 70 mya — page 18

Triceratops (try-SER-uh-tops) *Three horned face*, 26 ft. North America, 68–66 mya	page 19	**Pavo** (PAH-vo) *Latin name for peafowl* Blue peafowl, 84 in. Asia	page 20
Gallimimus (GAL-uh-mime-us) *Fowl mimic*, 20 ft. Asia, 75–66 mya	page 19	**Phoenicopterus** (fee-nuh-COP-ter-us) *Blood-red feathered* American flamingo, 57 in. Caribbean	page 21
Mononykus (muh-NON-ih-kus) *Single claw*, 3½ ft. Asia, 70 mya	page 19	**Bubo** (BYEW-bo) *Latin name for owl* Great horned owl, 22 in. North and South America	page 21
Rativates (rat-iv-ATE-eez) *Ratite (flightless bird) foreteller*, 11 ft. North America, 76 mya	endpaper	**Acryllium** (ah-krih-LEE-um) *Pointed feather* Vulturine guineafowl, 24 in. Africa	page 21
Parasaurolophus (par-a-sore-OL-uh-fus) *Like a crested lizard*, 25 ft. North America, 76–73 mya	endpaper	**Leptoptilos** (lep-TOP-tih-lus) *Delicate feathers* Marabou stork, 59 in. Africa	page 21
Camarasaurus (KAM-uh-ruh-sore-us) *Chambered lizard*, 60 ft. North America, 155–145 mya	endpaper	**Meleagris** (mel-ee-AH-griss) *Spotted like a guineafowl* Wild turkey, 49 in. North America	page 22
Buceros (BYEW-sir-os) *Horned like an ox* Rhinoceros hornbill, 49 in. Asia	page 20	**Dryocopus** (dry-oh-KOPE-us) *Tree cutter* Pileated woodpecker, 19 in. North America	page 22
Cathartes (ka-THAR-teez) *Cleanser* Turkey vulture, 28 in. North America	page 20	**Ardea** (AR-dee-uh) *Ancient Greek for fire* Great blue heron, 38 in. North America	page 22

Callipepla (ka-lih-PEH-pla) page 27
Beautifully adorned
California quail, 11 in.
North America

Balearica (ba-lee-AR-ih-kuh) page 27
From the Balearic Islands
Grey-crowned crane, 40 in.
Africa

Rallus (RAL-us) page 27
Slender
King rail, 19 in.
Eurasia

Amblyornis (am-blee-OR-nus) page 27
Dull bird
Vogelkop bowerbird, 13 in.
Asia, Oceania

Fregata (free-GAH-ta) page 28
Fast warship
Magnificent frigatebird, 39 in.
South America

Menura (meh-NUR-uh) page 28
Moon tail
Superb lyrebird, 35 in.
Australia

Gavia (GAH-vee-uh) page 28
Seabird
Common loon, 36 in.
North America

Cacatua (ka-ka-TOO-uh) page 28
Malay name for cockatoo
Sulphur-crested cockatoo, 14 in.
Australia

Ramphastos (ram-FAST-ahs) page 29
Curved beak
Toco toucan, 24 in.
South America

Haliaeetus (hal-ee-EE-uh-tus) page 29
Latin name for sea eagle
Bald eagle, 40 in.
North America

Recurvirostra page 29
(reh-curv-uh-RAH-struh) *Backward-bending bill*, Pied avocet, 18 in.
Eurasia

Eudocimus (yew-DAH-sih-mus) page 29
Glorious, excellent, and esteemed
Scarlet ibis, 24 in.
South America

Pelecanus (pell-eh-KAN-us) page 29
Axe,
Great white pelican, 60 in.
Eurasia, Africa

Aptenodytes (ap-ten-uh-DIE-teez) page 40
Unwinged diver
Emperor penguin, 45 in.
Antarctica

Apteryx (AP-teh-riks) page 40
Without wings
North Island brown kiwi, 28 in.
New Zealand

Struthio (STROOTH-ee-oh) page 40
Big sparrow
Common ostrich, 98 in.
Africa

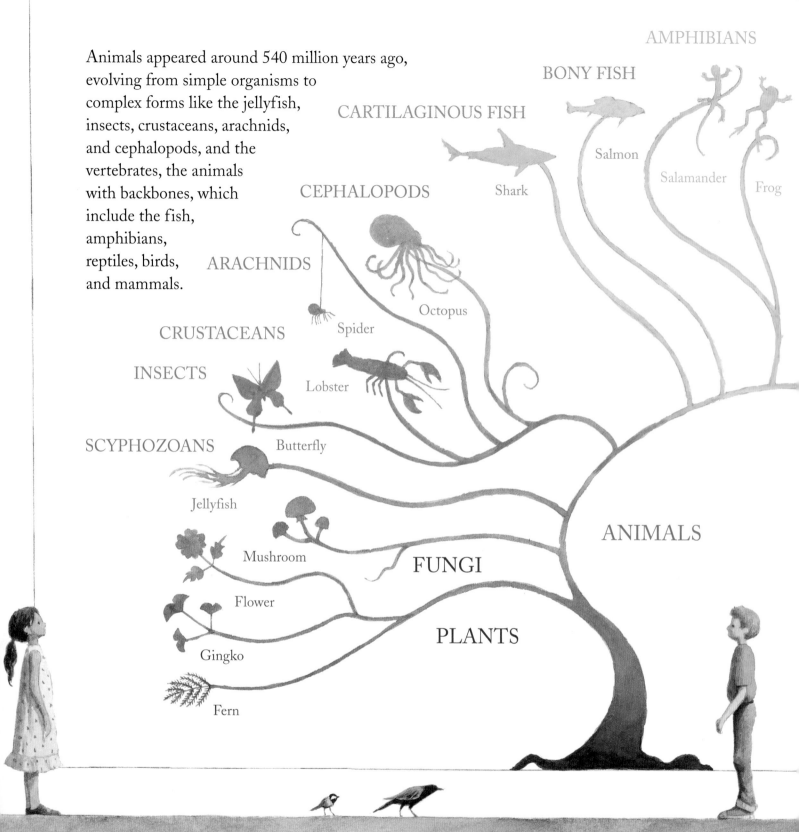

Animals appeared around 540 million years ago, evolving from simple organisms to complex forms like the jellyfish, insects, crustaceans, arachnids, and cephalopods, and the vertebrates, the animals with backbones, which include the fish, amphibians, reptiles, birds, and mammals.

AMPHIBIANS

BONY FISH

CARTILAGINOUS FISH

CEPHALOPODS

Salmon

Salamander

Frog

Shark

ARACHNIDS

Octopus

CRUSTACEANS

Spider

INSECTS

Lobster

SCYPHOZOANS

Butterfly

Jellyfish

Mushroom

ANIMALS

FUNGI

Flower

PLANTS

Gingko

Fern

Dinosaurs first appeared around 228 million years ago, sharing a common ancestor with the flying pterosaurs. As the dominant land animal, the dinosaurs spread to every continent on Earth and grew into an astonishing number of shapes and sizes. Birds appeared around 100 million years ago, as one of the feathered dinosaurs in the Theropod group that included the mighty Tyrannosaurus, the swift Velociraptor, the beaked Oviraptor, and the flying Archaeopteryx.

THE TREE of LIFE
4 Billion Years of Evolution

For around 70 million years, before the first dinosaur appeared, the largest land animals on Earth were the synapsids. Sharing a common ancestry with the reptiles, synapsids were the ancestors of all mammals, including humans.

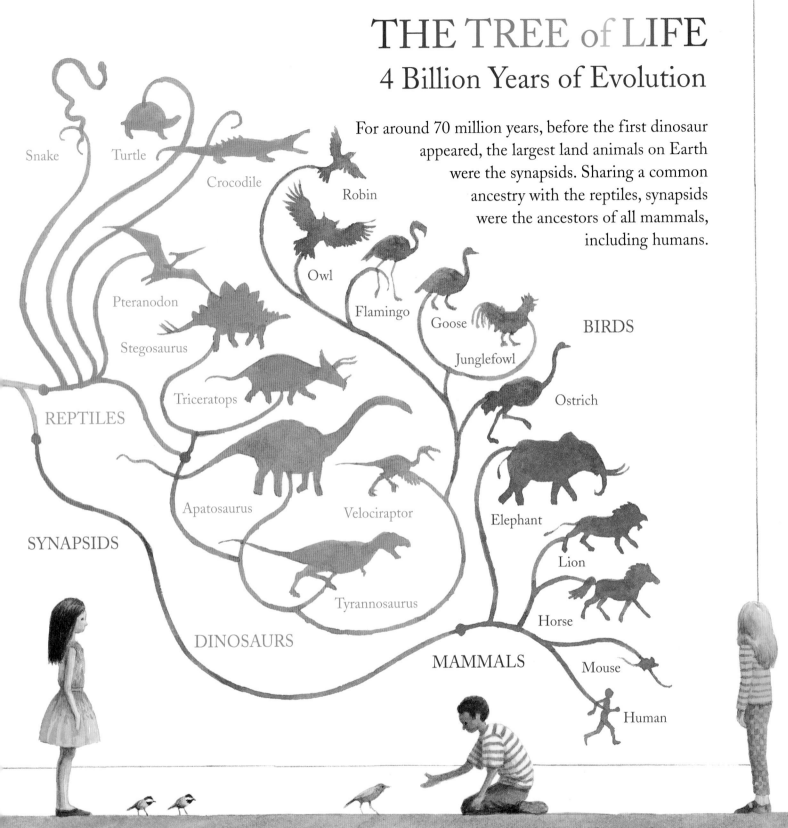

Snake
Turtle
Crocodile
Robin
Owl
Pteranodon
Flamingo
Stegosaurus
Goose
Junglefowl
BIRDS
Triceratops
Ostrich
REPTILES
Elephant
Apatosaurus
Velociraptor
Lion
SYNAPSIDS
Horse
Tyrannosaurus
DINOSAURS
MAMMALS
Mouse
Human

Feathers are modified reptilian scales that allowed the birds to take to the skies. The last dinosaur became extinct around 66 million years ago, except for a number of toothless, beaked, and feathered birds in ancient South America. Today around 10,000 species of birds inhabit the world, ranging in size from the giant ostrich to the tiny hummingbird. With a population of around 400 billion, they adorn the earth with the beauty of their colors and patterns, and fill the air with their song.

To three old dinosaurs—Bill, Doug, and Tom

The author wishes to thank Michael K. Brett-Surman, PhD, for his expert advice in assuring the accuracy of both text and illustrations.

Neal Porter Books

Text and illustrations copyright © 2019 by Dennis Nolan
All Rights Reserved
HOLIDAY HOUSE is registered in the U.S. Patent and Trademark Office.
Printed and bound in April 2019 at Toppan Leefung, DongGuan City, China.
The artwork for this book was made with transparent watercolor on watercolor paper.
Book design by Dennis Nolan
www.holidayhouse.com
First Edition
1 3 5 7 9 10 8 6 4 2

Library of Congress Cataloging-in-Publication Data

Names: Nolan, Dennis, 1945– author.
Title: Dinosaur feathers : from dinosaurs to birds / Dennis Nolan.
Description: First edition. | New York : Neal Porter Books/Holiday House,
    [2019] | Audience: Grade K to 3. | Audience: Ages 6 to 9. | Includes
    bibliographical references.
Identifiers: LCCN 2018042406 | ISBN 9780823443307 (hardcover)
Subjects: LCSH: Dinosaurs—Juvenile literature. | Birds—Origin—Juvenile
    literature.
Classification: LCC QE861.5 .N65 2019 | DDC 567.9—dc23
LC record available at https://lccn.loc.gov/2018042406

Additional reading: Among the many dinosaur books available, the author found these to be most helpful.

Children's Encyclopedia of Dinosaurs, Michael K. Brett-Surman, Weldon Owen, Australia, 2010.

Dinosaurs, Thomas R. Holtz Jr., Random House, New York, 2007.

Dinosaurs—The Grand Tour, Keiron Pim, The Experiment, New York, 2013.

Feathered Dinosaurs: The Origin of Birds, John Long and Peter Schouten, CSIRO, Australia, 2008.

The Princeton Field Guide to Dinosaurs, Gregory S. Paul, Princeton University Press, New Jersey, 2016.

The author also consulted inspirational paintings by paleo-artists that breathe life into dinosaurs including:

Charles R. Knight, John Sibbick, Raúl Martín, Peter Schouten, Julius Csotonyi, among others.

The bones of dinosaurs and their reconstructions in murals and displays may be found in many natural history museums, including:

American Museum of Natural History, New York, NY
Dinosaur Journey Museum, Museum of Western Colorado, Fruita, CO
Field Museum of Natural History, Chicago, IL
Peabody Museum of Natural History, New Haven, CT
Rocky Mountain Dinosaur Resource Center,
    Colorado Springs, CO
Smithsonian Museum of Natural History,
    Washington, D. C.
Wyoming Dinosaur Center, Thermopolis, WY